DRESSING UP

Devised and illustrated by
Clare Beaton

Kingfisher Books

Contents

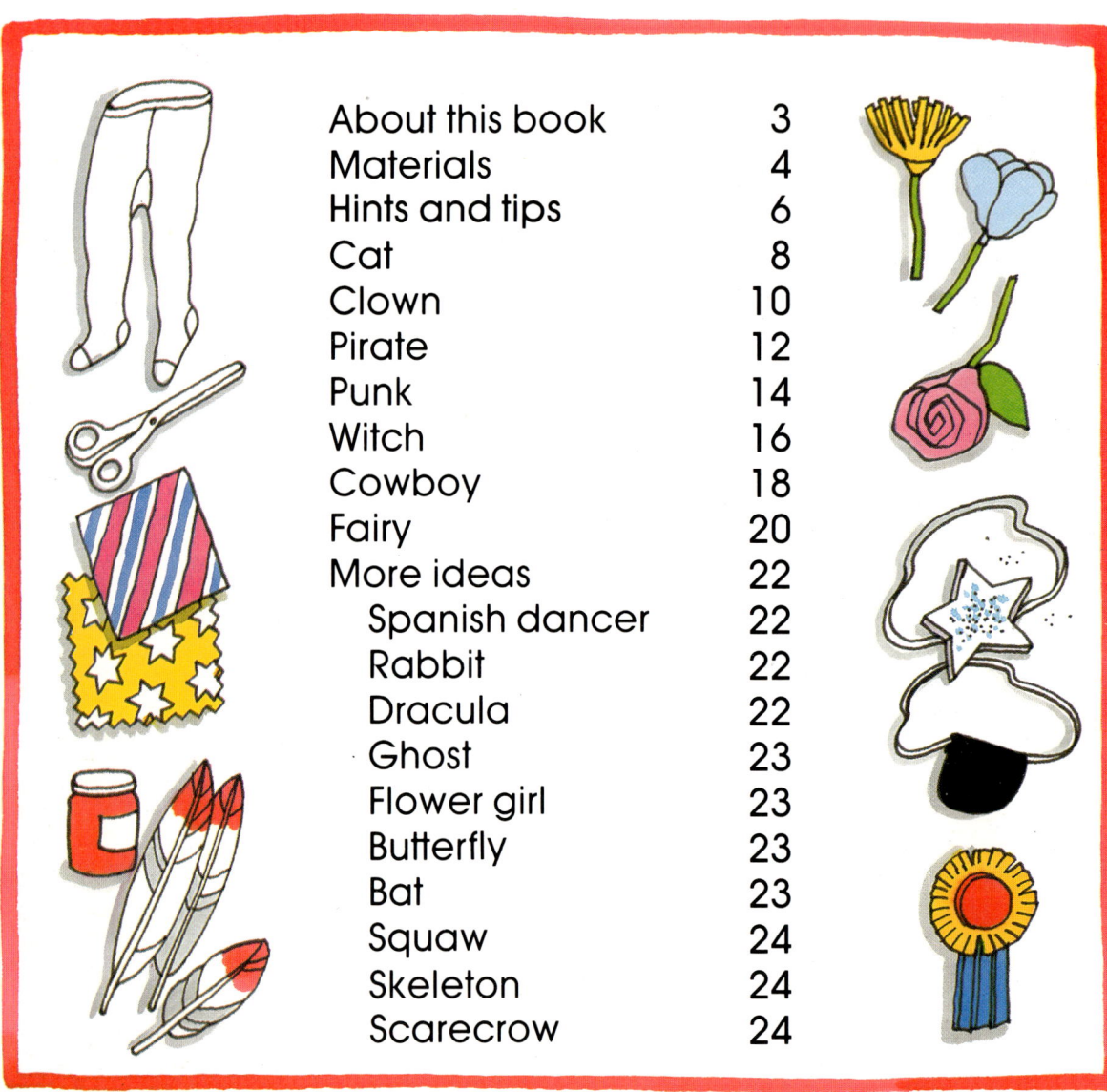

About this book	3
Materials	4
Hints and tips	6
Cat	8
Clown	10
Pirate	12
Punk	14
Witch	16
Cowboy	18
Fairy	20
More ideas	22
Spanish dancer	22
Rabbit	22
Dracula	22
Ghost	23
Flower girl	23
Butterfly	23
Bat	23
Squaw	24
Skeleton	24
Scarecrow	24

Produced for Kingfisher Books by Tony Potter, Times Four Publishing Ltd

Conception and editorial: Catherine Bruzzone, Multi Lingua

Kingfisher Books, Grisewood & Dempsey Ltd Elsley House, 24-30 Great Titchfield St, London W1P 7AD

First published in 1990 by Kingfisher Books
Copyright © 1990 Times Four Publishing Ltd
All rights reserved.
No part of the publication may be reproduced, stored in a retrieval system or transmitted by any means, electronic, mechanical, photocopying or otherwise, without the prior permission of the publisher.

Typeset by TDR Photoset, Dartford
Colour separations by RCS Graphics Ltd
Printed in Spain
British Library Cataloguing in Publication Data
Beaton, Clare
  Dressing up
  1. Children. Dressing-up
  I. Title II. Series
  646'.30
ISBN 0 86272 510 0

About this book

This book will show you some easy and fun ideas for your dressing up. There are step-by-step instructions for seven main costumes and outlines for lots more at the end of the book.

On the left-hand pages, there are four simple steps to follow:

On the right-hand pages, there is the finished costume with some extra suggestions for you to try:

The simplest costumes are at the beginning of the book and the more complicated ones at the end. You should be able to find most of the materials you need in your home. Look at pages 4-7 for some helpful hints.

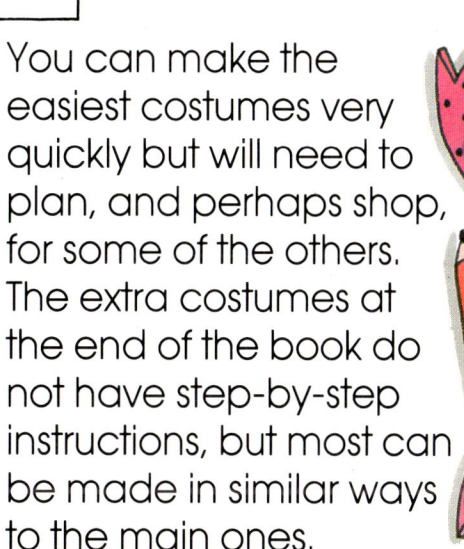

You can make the easiest costumes very quickly but will need to plan, and perhaps shop, for some of the others. The extra costumes at the end of the book do not have step-by-step instructions, but most can be made in similar ways to the main ones.

Warning

With this book, older children should be able to make all but the most complicated costumes on their own. However, they may need adult help occasionally and younger children will need help and supervision. It is worthwhile teaching children to use tools such as craft knives correctly and safely right from the start. Take special care with tools like scissors, knives and staplers and use non-toxic children's glue and paint.

Take extra care where you see this symbol:

Materials

Keep a dressing up box out of which you can take clothes and put together different outfits. Collect old clothes, hats and shoes from your own family and friends. Buy clothes from jumble sales and charity shops.

Even old curtains, bedspreads and sheets come in useful. Remember you can cut up outgrown or old clothes to make new costumes, they don't have to be used as they are.

Fur fabric looks wonderful made into hats, cloaks and cavemen costumes.

Use old tights as shown in the picture below to make the basic shape for a hat. Decorate the hat by adding things such as plastic flowers or scraps of material.

Make cloaks by pinning the top of skirts or curtains around your neck.

Pull on to head and tie legs.

Wash old tights. They can be useful as masks and hats as well as on your legs!

Nightdresses make lovely evening dresses.

In a box keep a selection of old cardboard boxes, wallpaper, wool, cardboard tubes, beads and scraps of material.

Net curtains make wonderful wedding veils and dresses.

Keep a box or tin with a lid for your toy jewellery and also collect old necklaces, rings, brooches and so on.

Hints and tips

A sewing basket will have lots of things you need, such as scissors, pins, needles and thread, but always ask the owner first! Also, keep a store of elastic, buttons, ribbon, braid, safety-pins and anything decorative and fun that might come in useful.

Keep ribbons and trimmings from presents and chocolate boxes.

Pinking shears are scissors that cut with a zigzag. They stop material from fraying and make a pretty edge.

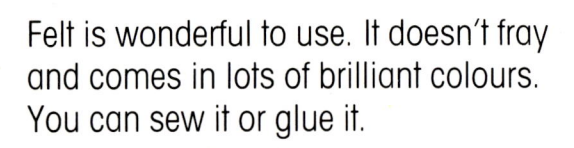

Felt is wonderful to use. It doesn't fray and comes in lots of brilliant colours. You can sew it or glue it.

A sewing machine is useful but is not essential and is best used only by an adult. Hand sewing will do fine.

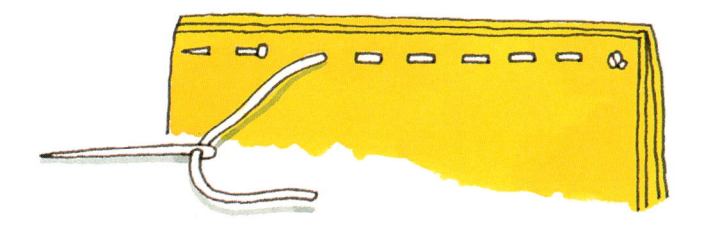

A running stitch is the easiest way to sew material together. Pin the pieces together and push the needle in and out in a straight line.

Make your own fringes by cutting material which doesn't fray, such as felt or paper, with even slits.

Don't cut right to the end but leave room for sewing on to the costume.

Overstitch
Pin
Knot the cotton at the end.

You can use sticky tape, glue, staples and safety-pins instead of sewing if you are in a hurry. If you use a stapler, make sure the staple ends are closed properly and don't leave staples lying around.

An overstitch is useful for sewing one piece of material on to another. Push the needle in and under.

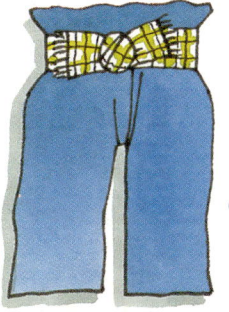

Safety pin to join elastic instead of sewing.

Glue on patches or decorations.

Cat

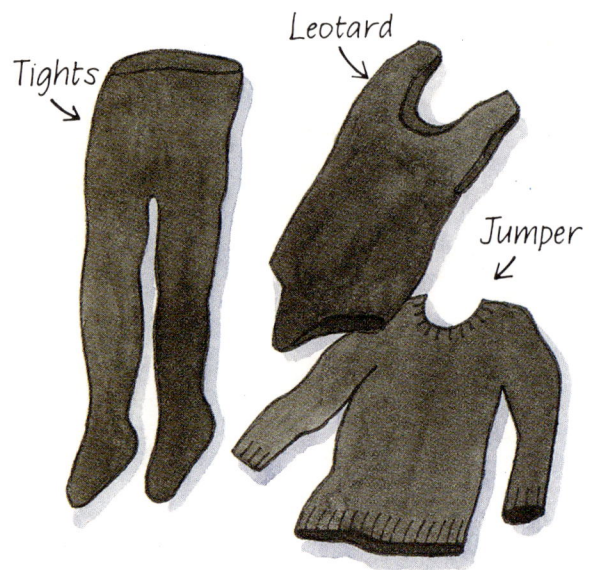

Tights *Leotard* *Jumper*

Fold

1 Collect any black clothes (or white clothes if you want to be a white cat).

2 Make ears from two triangles of black paper and two pink. Stick them to a hair band.

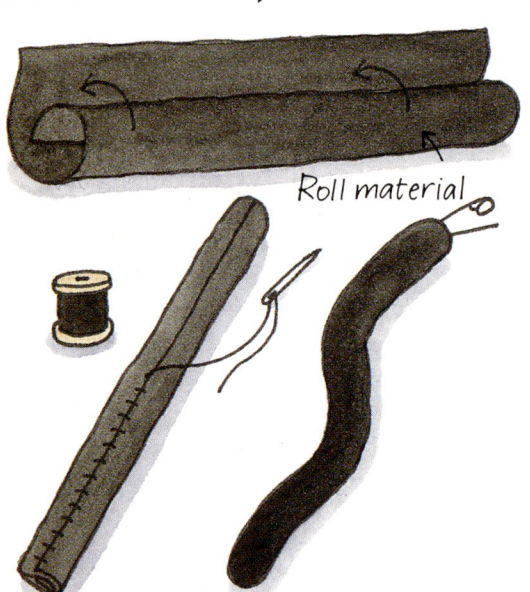

Roll material

3 Make a tail by rolling up a length of material. Sew along the join and pin on.

4 Use face paints to paint on a nose and whiskers.

8

Wear black gloves or mittens if you have any..

Add a pussy cat bow made out of a spare piece of material.

Make a paper fish for your tea!

Clown

Tie thin elastic through holes

1 Collect clothes that are either too big or too small. Try on a mixture to see what they look like.

2 Make a tiny hat out of a yoghurt pot and paper plate or circle of card.

3 Sew or glue patches on the clothes. Cut short some old trousers.

4 Use face paints to make up as a clown and hair gel for a crazy hair style.

You could buy or make a paper wig and wear a hat made from a decorated yoghurt pot.

Glue a paper flower on some wire.

Safety-pin on a joke flower water squirter.

Sew some bright buttons on and attach some braces.

You could use large boxer shorts instead of cut-down trousers.

Use coloured laces or ribbons in huge lace-up shoes.

11

Pirate

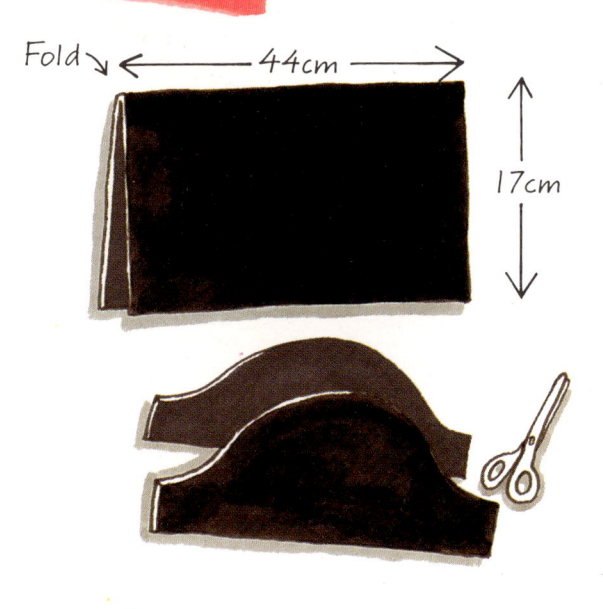

1 You will need a pair of old trousers, a leather belt, a T-shirt and scarf.

Cut jagged bottoms

2 Make a hat. Cut two hat shapes out of black card.

Fold ← 44cm → 17cm

3 Paint a skull and cross-bones on the front of the hat, or cut them out of white paper.

Glue skull and cross-bones to front.
Glue together

4 Lastly, make an eyepatch out of black card threaded with thin elastic.

Dirty smudges of face paint
Elastic
Card

Make a cutlass from card.

Make a treasure map out of paper. Colour it brown with cold tea.

Safety-pin a toy parrot on your shoulder.

Tear the edges to make the map look old.

Use the leather belt to hold up your trousers!

Sew or glue on some bright patches

Curtain ring earrings

You could tie the scarf around your head instead of the hat.

13

Punk

Black is best

1 Collect old clothes such as tights, jeans, vests, jumpers and T-shirts.

2 Try some of the clothes on in layers. Take them off, then very carefully cut some holes in them.

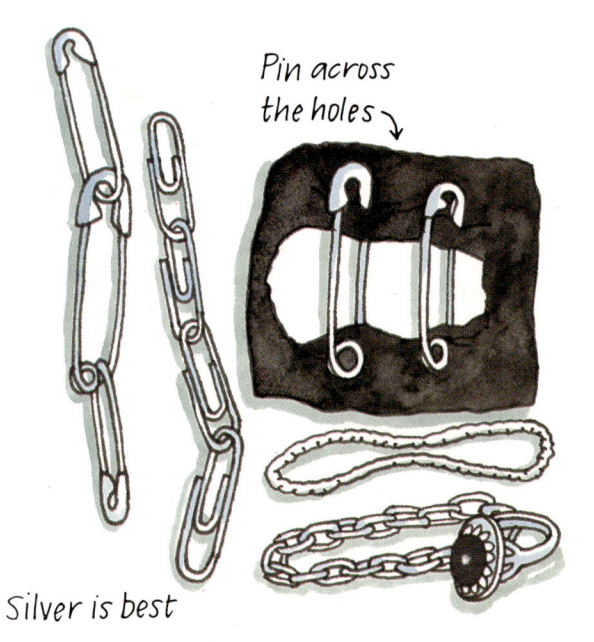

Pin across the holes

Silver is best

3 Next, decorate the clothes with safety pins, chains, paper clips or jewellery.

4 Use black to colour your eyes, mouth and nails. Use gel and coloured hairspray.

Make a Mohican haircut by taping crêpe paper along the centre of a swimming hat or the foot of a pair of tights.

Tie a black or Dayglo shoe lace or chiffon piece in your hair.

Put stick-on jewels in your ears and nose.

Draw pretend tattoos with blue and red washable felt-tips or face paints.

Tattoos to copy

Write on the clothes.

Witch

1 Make a tie-on skirt from a piece of black material (or an old skirt).

2 Make a cloak in the same way and glue on gold and silver stars.

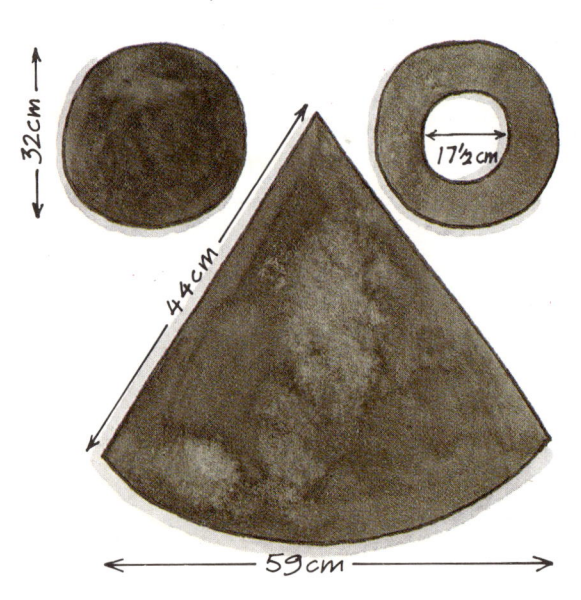

3 Cut a hat brim and cone from black paper. Cut a head-size hole in the brim.

4 Cut a fringe with scissors around the bottom of the cone. Then tape the parts together.

← 43 cm →

Make a wig to stick inside your hat by cutting foil or green or black crêpe paper into a fringe.

Make a broom from twigs tied onto a bigger stick or broom handle

Decorate hat.

Colour your hands and face with green face paint.

Take a toy cat with you.

Hang toy creepy crawlies around you.

17

Cowboy

35cm
40cm
Cut the same shape for the back and front.

Cut front down middle

1 You will need jeans, a checked shirt and a pair of wellington boots.

2 Waistcoat: use thick non-fray material, such as felt. Cut a back and two front pieces.

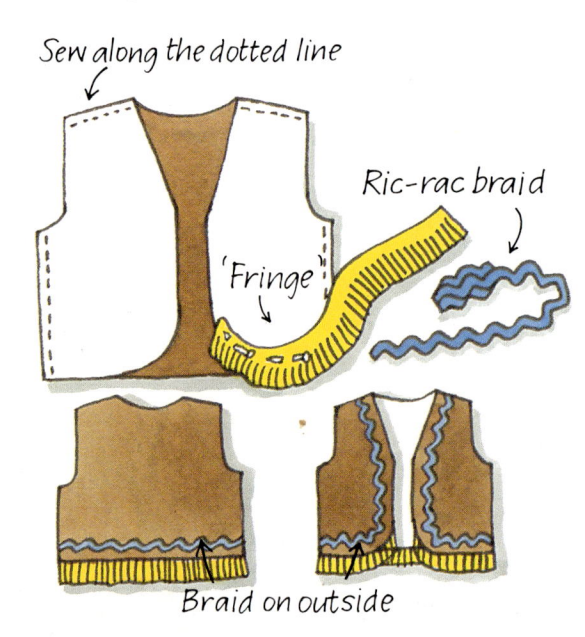

Sew along the dotted line

Ric-rac braid

'Fringe'

Braid on outside

Use pinking shears if you have some.

Sew, safety-pin or glue to waistcoat.

3 Sew the pieces together on the inside and sew on a fringe. Sew on the braid.

4 Sew, safety-pin or glue three pieces of coloured felt together to make a rosette.

Buy a cowboy hat or wear an old felt hat.

Tie a spotted hankie around your neck.

Try different shapes or colours.

Make a sheriff star out of silver card. Tape a safety pin on the back.

Cowgirl

Decorate a plain skirt and wear it instead of jeans.

19

Fairy

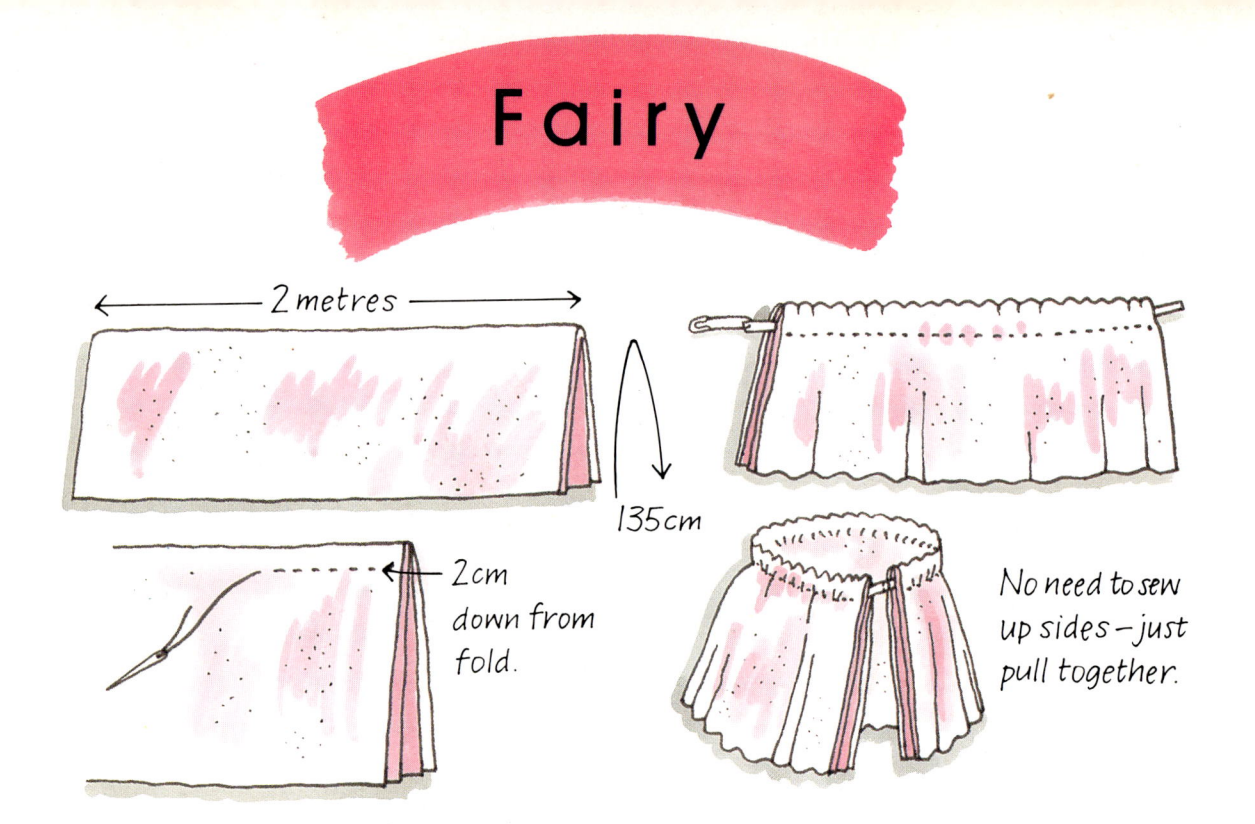

← 2 metres →

↕ 135cm

2cm down from fold.

No need to sew up sides – just pull together.

1 Skirt: fold two pieces of net of different colours and sew along the fold.

2 Measure some elastic around your waist and thread it through the gap.

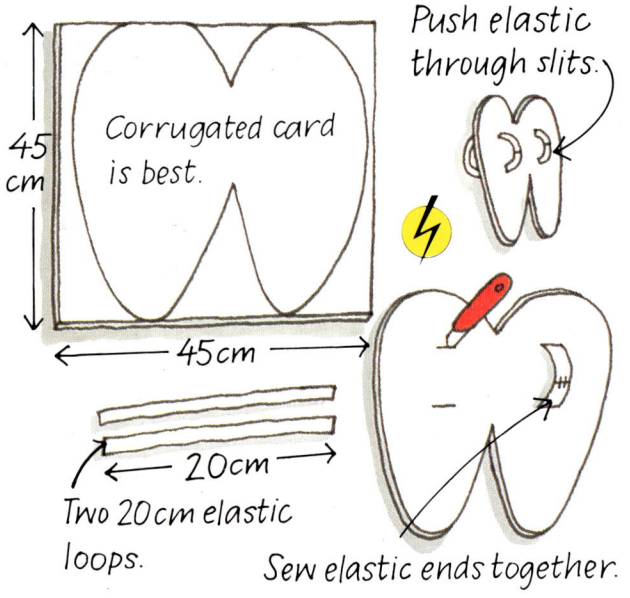

45cm

Corrugated card is best.

Push elastic through slits.

← 45cm →

← 20cm →
Two 20cm elastic loops.

Sew elastic ends together.

Card

3 Cut a pair of wings out of card. Paint them white. Cut 4 slits for the loops.

4 Cut two silver or gold stars. Tape one on a stick and one on elastic.

Glue on some sparkly glitter.

Use body glitter on your cheeks and shoulders.

Wear a sleeveless top or leotard.

Add more layers and colours of net for a fuller skirt.

Flower Fairy

Make a hat and green leaves for your waist out of green crêpe paper or material and net.

21

More ideas

If you enjoyed making the main costumes, try a few more!

There are no step-by-step instructions for these costumes but you can use many of the same techniques as the main ones. Look back at the page number shown in a circle like this: (16)

There are also some extra ideas shown for accessories you can make, such as castanets.

Flower in your hair.
Castanets
Bracelets
Sew skirt layers on to a petticoat

Spanish dancer (16) (20)
Make or find a long full skirt and shawl.

Mask
Glue on cotton wool.

Rabbit (4)
Make an ear mask and a tail. Paint a nose and whiskers.

Teeth made from washed yoghurt pot plastic.
Paper bat on wire or string.

Dracula
Wear a black suit and white shirt. Paint your face green.

Chain to rattle.

Cut eye holes in a white sheet.

Use real, plastic or paper flowers.

Ghost
Cut eye holes in a white sheet.

Flower girl ⑯ ⑳
Wear a blouse and skirt. Carry a basket.

Bend pipecleaners or add beads to ends.

Bead

Paint a pattern on net.

Cut black material this shape.

Add bat ears.

Sew on loops of elastic or tape.

Card ears.

Fold and glue.

Butterfly
Wear a leotard and tights. Make wings and antennae.

Bat ④
Wear a black leotard and tights. Make wings and ears.

23

Make headbands from paper.

Stick feather with tape.

Paint your face.

Plait your hair.

Tie a doll wrapped in cloth to your back.

Necklace

Draw patterns on the dress.

Cut a fringe.

Squaw (18)
Decorate a pinafore dress and cut a fringe. Wear moccasins, armbands and a headband with a feather.

Cover hair with a swimming hat.

Use face paints to paint a skeleton face.

Straw sticking out of clothes.

Tie string around trouser bottoms.

Skeleton (4)
Paint bones on black clothes with white paint.

Scarecrow (10)
Wear old clothes. Stick straw in your hair.